PRAYERS FOR BOYS
AND GIRLS

Given to _____

On this _____ day of _____

By _____

With this special message . . .

_____

_____

_____

PRAYERS FOR BOYS AND GIRLS

Illustrations by

Sam Butcher

Prayers by

Debbie Butcher Wiersma

Publishers since 1798

THOMAS NELSON PUBLISHERS

Nashville

CONTENTS

THANK YOU, GOD

FOR MY BODY

I like how you made me, God. I'm glad you gave me two strong legs. I'm glad you gave me arms with hands and fingers. If I had four legs like a bunny, I wouldn't be able to throw a ball or hold a popsicle. And if I didn't have fingers, I wouldn't be able to write letters or draw pictures. I have two pretty eyes to see things close up and far away. I have a nose to smell my favorite food. My mouth has lots of teeth to chew my food. I have ears to hear the birds sing and to hear when Mom calls me for dinner. But the best thing about me is that I have a mind to think and to decide what I want to do. Thank you, God, for making me as I am. Amen.

FOR MY BED-TIME FRIEND

Thank you, God, for my soft, cuddly bed-time friend. I like to feel his soft, furry ears. If it's dark in my room, I'm not afraid as long as my friend is there. Sometimes when I'm sad, I bury my face in his tummy and cry. He makes me feel better. He's been my friend for so long, I don't remember being without him. Thank you for giving me a special friend. Amen.

FOR BIRDS

Thank you, God, for making birds. I laugh when I see them flying up and down and turning circles in the air. When birds are way up in the sky, they make me think of angels. The very best thing about birds is their song. Thank you, God, for the birds that sing to me. Amen.

FOR MY FRIENDS

My friends are very important to me. They make me laugh when I don't feel happy. They go places with me and play my favorite games. My friends can be trusted to keep all my secrets. When we're together, we always have so much fun. Thank you for giving me such good friends. Amen.

13

FOR MY PET

Thank you for my pet, dear Lord. Some of my friends have dogs or cats. Some have fish or birds. Some even have snakes or lizards for pets. My pet is the perfect pet for me. I can take care of her and love her, and I can tell how much she loves me. When I have the very worst kind of day, I come home and see my pet do something funny, and all my bad feelings go away. A smile comes to my face. I just want to thank you for my pet. Amen.

FOR THE RAIN

Thank you for the rain, God. Sometimes I feel sad when it rains, because I can't go outside to play. Then I think about all of the good things rain does. Rain waters the flowers and grass in my yard. Rain gives the trees a drink. Rain waters the farmers' crops. When I think of all these good things about rain, I'm happy instead of sad. Oh, I almost forgot the very best part about rain—it makes mud puddles for splashing. Thank you for letting it rain, God. Amen.

FOR MY FAMILY

Thank you, God, for my family. I think I have the best family in the world. Sometimes we have disagreements and sometimes we argue. But I always know my family loves me. We help each other out with problems, and my family always seems to understand when I'm feeling sad. I've had lots of fun times with my family. As long as I'm with them, I'm happy. God, I'm glad you decided to give me to this family. Amen.

17

I DON'T FEEL GOOD
ABOUT WHAT I'VE DONE

ABOUT LYING

I told a lie today, God. It didn't seem like a big lie. It didn't seem like it would hurt to tell one little lie. But it did hurt, God. It hurt me to know that I lied. Even if no one ever finds out, I will always know. Please help me to tell the truth from now on.

If I want to tell a lie, please remind me how awful it will make me feel. I want always to tell the truth so people will always believe what I say. Please forgive me for lying, God. Amen.

ABOUT TAKING SOMEONE'S TOY

I did a very bad thing today, God. I took a toy that didn't belong to me. I knew it was wrong, but I felt as if I just had to have that toy no matter what. I feel so bad about taking it, I can't think about anything else. I know I have to give the toy back, but I'm scared. What should I say? God, please forgive me for what I did, and please help me to give it back. Thank you. Amen.

ABOUT DISOBEYING

I disobeyed my parents today, God. They told me not to cross the big street near our home, but I did. I feel bad about doing that. It made Mom and Dad angry, but even worse than that, it made them sad. I disappointed them, because they trusted me to obey them. I don't want to make them feel that way again, God. Please help me to obey. Amen.

ABOUT CHEATING

Dear God, please forgive me for what I did today. I cheated on a paper at school, and I feel very bad about it. I didn't know the answer. I didn't want to get a bad grade, so I looked at someone else's answer and wrote it down. I know that cheating is wrong, but I just didn't think about it. I have to tell the teacher what I did and I need your help. Please help me to tell her the truth, and please help me never to cheat again. Amen.

25

ABOUT FIGHTING

I got in a fight today, God. Even though I said it was all the other boy's fault, and he said it was all mine, we were both to blame. Neither one of us had to fight if we hadn't wanted to. We were just so mad! I don't even like to fight, God. Fighting isn't the right way to settle anything. I would like to think that I'm smart enough to talk to someone about a problem instead of hitting them. I'm sorry that I hit that boy, God. Amen.

ABOUT HURTING
SOMEONE'S FEELINGS

I'm sorry about what I did today, God. I said a very mean thing to my friend, and it hurt her feelings. She looked as if she were going to cry. I wanted to take back what I said, but I was too embarrassed. Now I feel terrible. I have to tell her how sorry I am, or I'll just feel worse and worse. Please help her to forgive me. And please help me to think before I say something that could make someone feel bad. In your name, I pray. Amen.

I NEED YOUR HELP, GOD

WHEN I'M BORED

Dear God, I need your help today. It's rainy and wet outside, and I can't think of anything to do. I don't want to play with my toys. I don't want to read my books. I don't want to play with my pet. Please help me think of something fun to do. Thank you, God. Amen.

31

WHEN I ACT BOSSY

I wasn't nice to my friends today, God. I wanted everyone to play my favorite games. My friends said, "You're too bossy!" I think they might be right. Please help me to stop acting bossy, Lord. I know I am not better than everyone else. I might even enjoy playing their games. Amen.

WHEN I'M AFRAID

Please help me not to be afraid, God. When I go to bed at night, it's so dark. Everything looks different from the way it did during the day. My window looks scary with the street light shining through. Dark shadows are all over my room and everything is so quiet. It's like I'm the only one here. I know you're always with me, God, so I don't have anything to be afraid of. But when it's dark and quiet, I get scared anyway. Please help me remember that you're always right here, God, even on the darkest nights. Thank you. Amen.

WHEN SOMEONE
ISN'T NICE

A boy at school is a real bully, God. He teases me and picks on me all the time. Sometimes he scares me. Other times he says mean things. His words hurt me, God. They make me want to cry. I get a sick feeling in my stomach when I think about him. Sometimes I just want to hit him, but I can't because I think hitting is wrong. Please help me to find a way to get along with this boy. And, God, if he won't be nice to me, please take extra good care of me. Amen.

I WANT TO
PRAY FOR OTHERS

FOR CHILDREN WHO ARE HUNGRY

Dear God, some children will go to bed hungry tonight, and I want to pray for them. Some children's tummies never feel full enough. In the Philippines and China, some children get only rice to eat. It fills them up, but they don't get the vitamins they need, so they can't grow up to be strong and healthy. Some children in my country will be hungry tonight too. Their parents do not have money to buy enough food. I am very lucky to have all that I have, God, but I'd like to pray for other children. Please help them to have a better life. Amen.

39

FOR OLDER PEOPLE

Dear God, please take care of the older people in the world. Old people have had years of experiences, and yet no one seems to want to hear about them. It must be lonely to be old, God. Some old people have children, grandchildren, and even great grandchildren, but they never get to visit them. I can do something to help. I can bring the old people in my neighborhood cookies or help them get their groceries. But most important of all, I can visit with them and listen to their stories. Amen.

FOR PEOPLE WHO GET HURT

Dear God, I hear about wars in other countries, and I think of all the people who get hurt. They fight and fight, and no one seems to win. So many people are hurt or even dead because these people keep on fighting. I don't know why they can't just sit down and talk with each other as I do when I'm angry with someone. Maybe I'm too young to understand, but I do know people get hurt. Please take care of all the people on every side. Amen.

FOR POLICEMEN AND FIREMEN

I want to pray for the policemen and the firemen, God. They put themselves in danger to help people they don't even know. Firemen will go into a burning building to save a person who might be trapped. Policemen try to keep everyone safe by making them obey the rules and laws. Please take care of the policemen and firemen who take such good care of me. Thank you, God. Amen.

FOR MY MOM AND DAD

Dear God, being a parent must be really hard. You have to work to earn money so you can support our family. You have to keep our home clean and cook our meals. Sometimes by the end of the day, Mom and Dad look tired. Please take care of them. Thank you, God. Amen.

FOR PEOPLE WITHOUT A HOME

God, please help all of the people in the world without a home. I have a warm, safe place to live in, but some people don't. They live in old, broken buildings. Some of them even live on the streets. Please help these people to find a real home and a soft bed to sleep on. Thank you, Lord. Amen.

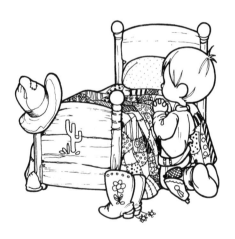

NOTE TO PARENTS

Jesus said, "Suffer the little children to come unto me. . . ." In these pages we offer twenty-three prayers, written specifically for children, with their needs, concerns, and feelings in mind. We know that when children pray, they do not use high-sounding phrases or complicated sentence structures. They use simple, direct, and honest language in their verbal relationship with God. Therefore these prayers are simple, direct, and open too.

It is our hope that these prayers will be read aloud to children at their normal prayer time. We hope that a discussion of the content of these prayers will be initiated at this time, and that children will be encouraged to express their thoughts and feelings freely. The prayers are not meant to be memorized. Instead it is hoped that they will be used as models to motivate children to create more personal and meaningful prayers of their own.